Star

Power

Eric Zweig

James Lorimer & Company, Ltd., Publishers
Toronto

James Lorimer & Company Ltd. acknowledges the support of the Ontario Arts Council. We acknowledge the support of the Government of Canada through the Book Publishing Industry Development Program (BPIDP) for our publishing activities. We acknowledge the support of the Canada Council for the Arts for our publishing program. We acknowledge the assistance of the OMDC Book Fund, an initiative of Ontario Media Development Corporation.

Cover design: Meghan Collins and Kate Moore

Library and Archives Canada Cataloguing in Publication

Zweig, Eric, 1963-
    Star power : the legend and lore of Cyclone Taylor / Eric Zweig. (Record books)

ISBN 978-1-55028-997-8 (bound). — ISBN 978-1-55028-995-4 (pbk.)

    1. Taylor, Fred, 1884-1979. 2. Hockey players — Canada — Biography. I. Title.
II. Series.

GV848.5.T39Z94 2007   j796.962092   C2007-904972-9

James Lorimer & Company Ltd., Publishers
317 Adelaide Street West, Suite #1002
Toronto, ON
M5V 1P9
www.lorimer.ca

Distributed in the United States by:
Orca Book Publishers
P.O. Box 468
Custer, WA USA
98240-0468

Printed and bound in Canada

Contents

For Barbara.
This is where we came in.

1 Print the Legend

His career began nearly 100 years before Sidney Crosby pulled on his first pair of skates. He played long before Wayne Gretzky or even Maurice "the Rocket" Richard. The sports pages were filled with stories about him. He drew crowds of fans everywhere he went. They cheered as he led dazzling rushes up the ice. He could score goals at one end and stop them at the other. He was the fastest skater anyone had ever seen. They called him Cyclone Taylor.

Cyclone played hockey when players first started getting paid. Giving people good money to play games was not very popular back then. The success of athletes like Cyclone helped change people's minds. He was professional hockey's first superstar.

Over the years, Cyclone's talent became legendary. It is now almost impossible to know what is truth and what is fiction. Many reporters exaggerated their stories about him. Exciting tales about sports stars made them seem more glamorous. They sold newspapers, as well as tickets to hockey games. The more the stories were repeated, the more people believed them. Even Cyclone himself couldn't always keep the facts straight.

Still, it wouldn't be fair to accuse people of lying. After all, there was no television when Cyclone was playing, so no one could check replays. There wasn't even radio. If you weren't at a game, there were only two ways to know what happened. People either told you what they saw or you read about it in the newspaper.

A line from an old Hollywood movie says: "When the legend becomes fact, print the legend." For a long time, that was all anyone could do. These days, it's possible to search very old newspapers online. They

PLAY FOR PAY

Paying athletes to play sports in Canada was not allowed until the early 1900s. Many people did not like the idea. They believed that sports were just for fun. They wanted all athletes to be amateurs — those who play for the love of their sport. Yet the men who owned teams and arenas were all getting rich. Hockey players knew this. Why shouldn't they make money too? So, in 1906, some leagues in Canada agreed to let teams sign players to professional contracts.

can be compared to see which facts line up and which do not. Each article provides another clue to what may have really happened. In this way, research is like detective work! The result is this book, which tries to recount Cyclone's story as truthfully as possible.

2 Off to a Fast Start

Before Cyclone became a legend, he was simply known as Fred Taylor. How confusing are the facts of Fred's life? Not even his birthday is known for sure!

A book written by his friend Eric Whitehead says that Fred was born on June 24, 1884. That is probably a mistake. Everything else written about him says he was born on June 23. Figuring out the year is trickier. Some agree with 1884 and others say 1883. But Fred's birthday was most likely June 23, 1885. That date appears on a plaque in Tara, the place where he was born.

Tara is a tiny town in southwestern Ontario. It is located just below the Bruce Peninsula, which divides Lake Huron from Georgian Bay. Only about 1,000 people live in Tara today. It was even smaller when Fred lived there.

Fred was the fourth of five children in his family. He had an older brother named Russell and three sisters. His two older sisters were Elizabeth and Harriet — who was called Hattie. His younger sister was Rose. There may also have been another two boys and a girl in the family who died as children. Sadly, this was common at that time.

Fred's father was Archibald Taylor, and his mother was Mary Bell. Archie, as his father was known, had a job selling farm equipment. He was a travelling salesman, so he was away from home a lot. Fred later recalled that his father was a kind person, but not really a family man. He liked to be alone, and sometimes he drank too much. As a result, Fred was much closer to his mother.

"She was deeply religious," he told Whitehead. "Yet she never preached to us. She taught us the basic good rules of living by example, and hoped we'd follow them."

Many of Mary's beliefs did influence her children. For example, Fred never smoked and he never drank alcohol. He rarely used swear words.

Perhaps his mother was a good athlete too. Archie definitely was not. Outside of fishing, Archie didn't care much for sports. Neither did Russell or Elizabeth. Only Hattie, Rose, and Fred showed interest in athletics. In fact, the first time Fred went on the ice, he wore a pair of Hattie's skates! "I just had to get out there and try it," he said. "So one day I stole my sister's skates and ran out with them. I got the dickens for it afterward, but it was worth it."

Fred was five years old at the time. He had been watching a man skating on a pond near the Sauble River. That man was Jack Riggs, a local barber. He was famous around town as a gifted speed skater. Jack noticed Fred watching him and offered him skating lessons. "My, that man was kind to me," Fred would later say. "He

YOU SAY IT'S YOUR BIRTHDAY

There is no official record of Fred's birth. He wrote "June 23, 1885" in letters he wrote to the Hockey Hall of Fame. That's the same date that appears on the plaque in Tara. It is also the date in the first newspaper story Fred wrote about his life. Yet there are other letters in his own handwriting saying he was born on June 23, 1884!

taught me to skate right there on the pond. Later, he took me out on the river. He'd get ahead and make me stretch out just enough to give me confidence."

Jack even bought Fred his first pair of skates. It was a late present for his sixth birthday. "I didn't know what a hero was in those days," Fred remembered. "I guess he was my first one."

In about 1891, the Taylor family left Tara. They moved 90 kilometres (56 miles) south to the small town of Listowel, Ontario. Soon Fred was skating on another river. Many years later, he described it in a story for the *Listowel Banner*. "My first hockey playing was on the Maitland River, under the stores on Wallace Street," he wrote. "We also played on the dam near the old Brewery ice house."

One place Fred didn't skate much as a boy was the Listowel Arena. "We were a poor family," he admitted. "My father only earned fifty or sixty dollars a month. Listowel certainly wasn't snobbish, but some folks were better off than others. We children living on the other side of the tracks did not attend the arena too often."

No matter where he skated, Fred loved to be on the ice. When he wasn't playing hockey, he skated for hours up and down the river. This helped develop his strength and stamina. He also started building his speed.

When Fred was about 16 years old, an ice show came to town. It featured a man named Norval Baptie — a world champion

BAPTIE ON BLADES

Norval Baptie was born in Bethany, Ontario. He grew up in the state of North Dakota. He won his first world title in 1895 when he was only 16. Over the next 25 years he won nearly 5,000 races ranging from 200 metres (220 yards) to eight kilometres (five miles).

speed skater. As part of the show, Norval held a contest. He promised a pair of skates to anyone who could beat him in a quarter-mile (400-metre) race. To even things up, Norval would skate backwards!

Fred's friends were sure he could beat Norval. So was Fred. "I always did think I could beat the other fellow," he told Whitehead. "No matter what."

In spite of this confidence, Fred was in awe of Norval: "He was the first world champion of any kind we had ever seen!" When Norval asked for a head start, Fred gave it to him. It only seemed fair. He learned soon enough why it was not.

"Each time I'd get close enough to pass him, he'd swing out just enough to block me," he recalled. "It was just a little shift of his hips. Right away I began to appreciate the art of skating backward. The trick was not the speed, but the balance. Right then and there I told myself that I was going to learn to become as good at it as he was. I could see its value to a hockey player."

Much later, people would swear that Fred could skate faster going backwards than most hockey players could going forward! But those days were still a long way off.

3 A Rising Star

Fred played many sports while growing up in Listowel. He was great at lacrosse and loved baseball and soccer too. Fred was an alternate player on the 1902 Listowel team that reached the final in the Western Football Association. Hockey was always his favourite sport, though.

Fred began playing hockey seriously around 1898. By 1901, the top local team was the Listowel Juniors. They won the Northern Hockey League championship that year. After that season, most of their older players retired. Fred was among the youngsters who took their places. No one knew what to expect of the young team. They made their town proud by winning the Northern Hockey League title again in 1902. The players were given medals for winning the championship. Fred kept his for the rest of his life.

1904 Listowel Hockey Team. Fred Taylor is second from the right.

Fred was now the best hockey player in Listowel. He was even attracting attention from newspapers in Toronto. The big city was 160 kilometres (100 miles) away. In a game story on February 6, 1902, the *Globe* reported: "Taylor was a star. He worked like a Trojan from start to finish." In 1903, Fred led Listowel to a third Northern Hockey League championship.

Hockey at this time was very different than it is today. Games had two 30-minute halves instead of three 20-minute periods. Players had to play the entire 60 minutes, unless someone was badly injured. On the other hand, there was an extra player on the ice. This seventh player was known as the rover. The rover lined up between the forwards and the defencemen. The defencemen were known as point and cover-point. The other positions were the same as in modern hockey.

Hockey in Canada was strictly amateur

when Fred was playing in Listowel. No one could be paid for playing. If a player took money, he could be banned from competing in any sport. Even so, after a good game Fred often found a few dollars tucked inside one of his boots. The money was from his many fans. It came in handy. When he was only 15, Fred had to quit school and get a job. He began working at the local piano factory. The $10 he made each month helped out, but times were still tough in the Taylor family. Hockey was a good way to forget those troubles.

Fred was not just the best hockey player on his team. He was also one of the youngest and smallest. Even when he was fully grown, Fred was only about 5'8" or 5'9". He weighed just 165 pounds. This made him a target that other teams would try to hit. It was never easy to catch the speedy little left-winger. When someone did, Fred was sent sprawling. To protect himself, he asked his mother to sew felt padding into his underclothes. He also tucked the hard material from women's corsets into his hockey pants! At first, the teasing he took was probably worse than the hits. Eventually, Fred's ideas about gear began to catch on.

In addition to playing in the Northern Hockey League, the Listowel Juniors also played in another league. The Ontario Hockey Association (OHA) was the top league in the province. It had dozens of teams in different divisions across Ontario. The Listowel Juniors had never won their

PROTECT YOURSELF

One story about Fred says that he began to add padding to his gear when he played hockey in Renfrew, Ontario, in 1910. The story claimed he got the idea in a harness shop when he saw how felt was used to cushion saddles for horses.

OHA division. People expected that to change in 1904.

Fred was 18 during the 1903–04 season. He was captain of the Listowel Juniors now, and he and his teammates began practising early. Their hard work paid off with plenty of wins. After a victory over the team from London, Ontario, the Listowel Banner declared: "Taylor is a whirlwind."

Listowel's biggest win of the OHA season came against Ingersoll. It was the middle of winter — January 4. The team from Ingersoll was very late arriving due to bad weather. The game didn't start until 11:15 at night. That did not put off the large crowd who waited to watch.

"The fans then were an amazingly hardy lot," Fred remembered. "It seems that the winters were much colder and longer then. The wind would howl and the temperatures would get down way below zero. Out they'd come in the bitter cold. They'd pack those drafty arenas and love every minute of it. They came on foot, by train, or in sleighs. They dressed in furs and sat under blankets. They rarely left before the final whistle."

The Listowel Juniors gave their fans plenty to cheer about. Some newspapers list the score as 23 to 5, though others say 24 to 5.

The Listowel Juniors finally won their

SNOW DAYS

The winter of 1904 was one of the worst ever in southwestern Ontario. January's heavy snow buried the train tracks. No mail reached Listowel for weeks. On January 26, 1904, a story appeared in Toronto's *Globe* newspaper. "The Listowel Juniors are snowed under," it said. "Three or four players have not yet got home from their last game. Those who are there got home on foot."

division. After two more playoff wins, it was on to the OHA junior championship game in Toronto. They lost to the Kingston Beechgroves, but the people of Listowel were still proud of their team. It had been a wonderful season.

Fred was now famous across his home province. For a star player from a poor family, hockey offered a chance for a better life. Even if teams couldn't pay Fred, there were other ways to reward a player. Teams often lured athletes by helping them find good jobs. That was probably the reason Fred decided to leave Listowel in the autumn of 1904.

Fred would later remember a telephone call from Billy Hewitt, the secretary of the OHA. He wanted Fred to play senior hockey for the Toronto Marlboros. "I was flattered," Fred told author Eric Whitehead. "I wanted to go. It was my chance to move up to big-time hockey."

Then Fred had second thoughts. He'd been born and raised in two small towns. Toronto suddenly seemed awfully big. "I liked Listowel," he said. "My home was there, and I had my job in the piano factory … I thanked Mr. Hewitt for asking me, but I said I wouldn't come."

Hewitt got very angry with Fred. "He told me straight out, 'if you won't play for the Marlboros, you won't play anywhere!'"

Hewitt was a powerful man in the

FAMOUS FAMILY

William "Billy" Hewitt was secretary of the OHA for 58 years! He was also the sports editor of the *Toronto Star* for 32 years. But he is not the most famous person in his own family. His son, Foster Hewitt, was one of hockey's first play-by-play announcers. He broadcast games on radio and television from 1923 to 1972. Both Billy and Foster are in the Hockey Hall of Fame.

OHA. He really could ban Fred from playing hockey in Ontario. But would he?

The story of Billy Hewitt may not have happened just as Fred recalled it. There do not seem to be any newspaper stories about the Marlboros trying to get him. However, there are many stories about other teams that were.

"Half a dozen clubs have claimed him," stated the *Woodstock Sentinel-Review*. The newspaper said if Fred wouldn't play for the Woodstock team, "he will not play [anywhere] in the OHA." Another threat!

The town of Thessalon was going all out to build a great team. "The most notable [addition] to the Thessalon forces is Grindy Forrester," the *Globe* reported. It went on to say that two other players were going to Thessalon. One of them was "Taylor of Listowel." The newspaper called him "one of the fastest players in his district last year."

HOCKEY PLAYERS AT OWEN SOUND

Taylor of Listowel Among the Crack Backs Secured by the Town Club.

includes Newbold and Paterson of Collingwood, point and goal men respectively. Boyce of Midland, Carscau of Orillia, Owen Sound, Oct 6.—The list of hockeyists available for the Owen Sound team, Taylor of Listowel, three good forwards. Leroy of Markham, a strong cover point, Teggart, Vail, and McDonald of Barrie; Armstrong of Thessalon, and death of Midland. The Wellingtons will amalgamate to strengthen the organization.

Hockeyist For Listowel.

Woodstock, Oct. 13.—The many friends of Percy Thornton will regret to hear of his departure from Woodstock. He has been connected with hockey and other sports here for the past two or three years, and in all he proved himself a good sport and an athlete of more than ordinary promise. He carries to Listowel the good wishes of hosts of friends in this city.

Quebec Team's Line-up.

Quebec, Oct 15.—The Quebec Hockey Club is commencing to organize for the winter's play, but nothing practical will be done until the close of the football season, as most of the hockey players are interested in kicking the pigskin. The hockey team will be considerably weakened by the loss of Stanley and Leader, who have gone to Winnipeg to re ice.

A new lot of players, however, are coming into existence, which will furnish good material to strengthen the team. Moran will again play in goal. Hogan and Power defence, and Jordan, Bosse, and Garneau on the forward line, and it is probable that Harold Blair will be chosen to succeed Stanley.

Cost of Stanley Cup Trip.

Winnipeg, Oct 14.—The annual meeting of the Winnipeg (Rowing Club) Hockey Club was held last night.

The club is managed by a committee of four with the captain, who co-operate with the officers of the Rowing Club. The committee elected and evening showed considerable new blood, all the old stalwarts but Charlie Johnstone retiring. The quartet are: C. W. Johnstone, C. Quinn, W. R. Bawlf, and A. H. E. Kent. Last

year's captain, Billy Breen, was re-elected by unanimous vote.

A satisfactory financial statement was presented by Secretary-Treasurer Harold Richards, showing the club with a balance of £6.30. The total receipts of the club for the season were $3,000.6. The trip after the Stanley Cup left the club with a deficit of over $500, which cut down the profits for the season materially. The club received nearly $1.50 for its share of the local games, and over $1.50 for the exhibition games, which included the Stanley Cup games and the dance with hat racing. The chief item in the expenditure was for traveling expenses, which aggregated nearly $1,000. A segment item in the expenses was one of $102 for doctors' fees.

Among the players of the champion team of last year who were at the meeting were Charlie Quinn, Percy Browne, Crawford Richards, Billy Bawlf, Billy Breen, and Clou'e Borland, while there was a great representation of the intermediates and juniors. Stanley of Quebec, who played lacrosse with the Minto during the season, was one of the old men present.

Hockey in Western Ontario.

The Woodstock Sentinel-Review says of the hockey situation:

"A question that will come up for discussion in this district of the O.H.A. this coming season is whether the clubs may senior or intermediate. Season after season the question is discussed, but the clubs split and finally go back to intermediate. In Galt they are anxious to go in the senior series, and Stratford is believed to be of the same mind. In Brantford they have been talking Stanley Cup and senior hockey for a month, but intermediate will be about their limit when it comes to facing the puck. One thing is certain, whether we play senior or intermediate, the class of hockey will be the same, as the same players will represent the different towns. Ingersoll, no doubt, friends putting an intermediate team on the ice, and are adverse to the senior proposition. If the groupings are the same this season as last, Ingersoll and Woodstock will not likely be in the same district. London, Ingersoll, and Wexford, who are all in favor of intermediate, could be in a group, while Stratford, Galt, Paris, Guelph, Woodstock, and Brantford, if the majority rule, will play senior.

"Seaforth is erecting a fine new hockey and skating rink. Seaforth was grouped with the senior club, and had a good team. Now that they are to have a new rink we may expect to see the Scotchmen with us again.

"Galt and the Canadian Soo team would like to have Pete Maltman as goal-tender, but if Pete stays in the game this winter he will likely be found here."

HE SOLD IT.

Gyer—"My brother has been greatly benefited by patent medicines."

Myer—"So? What kind did he take?"

Gyer—"Oh, he didn't take any. He's a druggist."

The first time Fred's name appeared in Listowel's newspaper was on March 7, 1901. On October 14, 1904, the Owen Sound Times *ran an article about which players were free to join the local team that year. Among the names was "Taylor of Listowel." The same story ran in the* Toronto Star *the next day (pictured above).*

When Fred finally left Listowel, he did go to Thessalon. He was given a job at the Queen's Hotel. He worked as a clerk, and was given a room to live in. There was time off for hockey practice. The children of Thessalon flocked to the rink to see their new young star in action. They marvelled at his speed and stickhandling. Fred was always friendly with the kids. Sometimes he offered them a nickel to help him lace up his skates before practice. Unfortunately, practising was the only thing Fred did in Thessalon.

A player had to ask the OHA if he could move to a new team in the league. The OHA wanted to be sure that a person had a real reason for moving to a new city. They didn't want people to jump from team to team. That would be against the amateur spirit. Shortly after Fred moved to Thessalon, he was told he wouldn't get the permit he needed. Hewitt really had banned him! Was it because he hadn't joined the Marlboros? Maybe. Or, maybe the team from Woodstock filed a protest. Whatever the reason, Fred could not play for Thessalon.

Hockey officials in Thessalon appealed the ruling. They were so sure the OHA would change its mind that they convinced Fred to stay in town. He kept practising with the team until his case came up again. The OHA made its final decision at a meeting on February 11, 1905. Fred could not play hockey anywhere in the province of Ontario.

4 Go West, Young Man!

Fred went home to Listowel. He did not have a job when he returned, but he joined the soccer team again as the goalie. In July, the team won the Western Football Association junior championship. Fred got even better news near the end of the summer. A senior hockey team wanted him to join them for the 1905–06 season. The team was in Portage la Prairie, Manitoba. Billy Hewitt and the OHA had no control over hockey in that province.

Fred wanted to go. When the letter came from Portage la Prairie, Fred talked it over with his family. His mother told him that if this was something he really wanted to do, he should do it. He decided to accept the offer.

It was against the rules to give Fred a salary, but he would get $25 a month in "pocket money" and a place to live. The team sent him a train ticket at the end of November. Portage la Prairie was 85 kilometres (53 miles) west of Winnipeg. It was the furthest Fred had ever been from home. With just 3,000 people, it wasn't much bigger than Listowel. Still, the hockey would be much better than anything he had played before. Teams from Winnipeg had won the Stanley Cup three times in the past 10 years. Teams from the nearby towns of Brandon and Kenora had challenged for the championship too.

Fred was worried about how he would play. He had not played a real game in a long time. "I needed a real challenge to get my confidence back," he recalled. "I figured I'd find it in the Manitoba league."

He did.

Fred played his first game in Portage la Prairie on December 27, 1905. It was almost a year to the day since he had been banned from playing hockey in Ontario. Maybe he was too eager to prove himself. He was usually a clean player, but he got into a fight with a Brandon player about one minute into the game. He then got into another fight and was kicked out. Portage la Prairie lost the game to Brandon.

Fred had played on the forward line against Brandon. He was switched to cover-point for the next game, against the Winnipeg Victorias. Point men needed to stay close to their goalie. Not the cover-point, though. Teams had started letting their cover-points carry the puck from end to end. They just had to be fast enough to get back and play defence. Fred was plenty fast. "He is one of the fastest men seen in these parts for some time," said the *Manitoba Free Press*. "His swift rushes were good for three goals."

Portage la Prairie beat the Victorias 11 to 8.

The next game was against the Kenora Thistles. The Thistles were defending league champions and one of the top teams in Canada. "I had worked myself into a nervous state wondering how I'd stack up against those fellows," Fred admitted. "I needn't have worried. It was one of those nights when I could do nothing wrong. Everything worked. I don't think I ever skated faster or moved better ... The crowd loved it."

Fred played rover in the game against the Thistles. The newspapers said he was one of the best players on his team. However, things could not have gone nearly as well as Fred remembered. Kenora beat Portage la Prairie 14 to 1!

Fred only played one more game for Portage la Prairie. On January 31, 1906, an article in the *Manitoba Free Press* reported that "Important Changes" had been made to the team. A new manager took over, and two players were cut. One of them was Fred.

Some stories claim that the Thistles wanted Fred to join them. Was an offer made after Portage la Prairie cut him? Did he quit to jump teams? In any case, Fred never did join the Thistles. Instead, he went south to another "Portage" — to Houghton, Michigan, on the shores of Portage Lake.

Houghton is in a part of Michigan known as "Copper Country." Copper mines made the whole area very wealthy.

Mining men were rugged, and they wanted exciting entertainment. Hockey was the perfect game for them during the long, cold winters.

The Portage Lake Hockey Club was run by Jack Gibson. A Canadian, he moved to Houghton in 1900. He was a dentist, but when people found out he played hockey, they asked him to join the team. Jack tried to get other Canadians to join the team, but Houghton was not the

BANNED BACK HOME

Like Fred, Jack Gibson was once banned by the Ontario Hockey Association. Gibson was playing for the OHA team in Berlin, Ontario, in 1898. He and his teammates were each given a $10 gold coin. It was a small reward for beating their rivals from Waterloo. This broke the OHA rules about amateur hockey. The entire Berlin team was kicked out of the league that year.

easiest place to get to or to live in. Local businessmen began paying Canadian players to come. In 1903, Portage Lake became the first professional team in hockey history. They were also the best in the United States.

Soon, teams in other American cities were paying Canadians to join their teams. In the winter of 1904–05, a pro hockey league was formed. It was called the International Hockey League (IHL). Portage Lake didn't win that year, but they spent much of the next season in first place. Then they starting slumping again. The team needed help.

On February 1, 1906, the *Toronto Star* reported that the Portage Lake Hockey Club had signed Fred. He was going to be paid $400 for the rest of the season. It was more money than he had ever seen in his life.

As Fred made the journey to

Houghton, he stared out of the window of the train at the bleak landscape. He was met at the station by a strong wind howling in off Portage Lake. The wind made the temperature feel even colder. Fred wasn't sure what he had gotten himself into. He was scared stiff. "I'd never felt so lonely in my life," he admitted.

Fred began to feel a lot better once he met some of his new teammates. One of them was a player he already knew: Grindy Forrester, from Thessalon. Grindy helped Fred feel at home in his new surroundings. After a week of practising with his new team, Fred was ready to play.

Fred played rover for Portage Lake. In his first game, he scored two goals in an 8 to 2 victory over the team from Calumet. The local newspaper admitted it wasn't a very good game, but it had lots of good things to say about Fred. "With the new man Taylor in charge of the attack, the

Portage Lake goalie had little work to do," it reported. "The goalie for Calumet was kept busy, especially with Taylor buzzing about him for most of the game … He is a whirlwind."

After another win over Calumet, the Portage Lake team hit the road. They travelled to Pittsburgh, Pennsylvania. Pittsburgh was one of the teams they were battling for first place. Pittsburgh won the first in the three-game series. Portage Lake won the next. Fred played well, but he didn't score in either game. He made up for it in the third match. "Taylor shot all three goals for Portage Lake," said the Houghton newspaper. "The final score was 3 to 2."

"Taylor was the king bee for the visitors," said the *Pittsburgh Leader*. Even though Fred had beaten their team, Pittsburgh fans cheered for him. "His work was so brilliant and beautiful to watch that the audience got to their feet with loud shouts and to blow their horns."

Portage Lake had just two games left in the season. They needed to win both to take the IHL championship — and they did. Fred got a hat trick in the final game to lead Portage Lake past Calumet again, this time 10 to 5.

After the season, Fred went home to Listowel. That autumn, some Canadian teams decided they had to start paying their players. Many of the stars in the IHL signed with Canadian teams, but Fred went back to Houghton. He played point for Portage Lake that year, and the team won another championship.

The 1906–07 season turned out to be the last one for the IHL. "It was a wonderful training ground," Fred said. "I was a far better player for my experience there. After that league, I knew I could handle anybody, anywhere."

Other people seemed to know it too.

Before long, teams across Canada were trying to sign him.

5 On to Ottawa

Fred returned to Listowel in the spring of 1907. He was becoming a local celebrity. People stopped him on the street just to say hello.

Fred lived at home with his family. He played lacrosse for the team in nearby Hanover. Before the summer was even half over, offers from hockey teams began to arrive.

The contract that Fred found most tempting came from the Ottawa Senators.

Other teams could pay more than the $500 the Senators were offering. But Ottawa could give Fred something even more important. The team would get him a job in the civil service of the Canadian government. With his hockey salary added to his job pay, he would make close to $1,000 that year. That was a decent wage for a young man in those days.

Fred knew the hockey season was only three months long. An injury could end his playing career at any time. A job in the civil service could turn into a real career. So, he took the Senators' offer. In the

SILVER SEVEN

Ottawa's Stanley Cup team of 1903 to 1905 is best known today as the Silver Seven. At the time, though, the team was usually called the Ottawas. The name Senators became common around 1907.

autumn of 1907, he moved to Ottawa to live, work, and play hockey.

The Ottawa Senators played in the Eastern Canada Amateur Hockey Association (ECAHA). Despite its name, the league did allow professional players. It was the best league in the world, and the Senators were one of the greatest teams in history.

Fred was under a lot of pressure. Ottawa had been the Stanley Cup champions in 1903, 1904, and 1905. The next two seasons had not gone as well. Now the team was trying to rebuild and were counting on Fred. He wasn't too worried. Fred knew he was good, and couldn't wait to show it. Unfortunately, he didn't get off to a good start.

The Senators' first game should have been easy. It was a disaster. Ottawa opened the 1907–08 season against the Quebec Bulldogs. The game was not even close.

Fred Taylor in his Ottawa Senators' uniform

Quebec won 8 to 1. The lopsided score wasn't the worst of it.

"What a rude shock!" said a story in the *Ottawa Journal*. "And our high-priced team, too!"

Fred was only making $500, but some of his teammates were making a lot more. The highest-paid was Tommy Phillips. Tommy had been the captain of the Kenora Thistles. He was one of the best players in Canada. In January of 1907, Tommy led Kenora to the Stanley Cup. Many teams wanted him after that. The Senators paid $1,600 to get him. At the time, it was the most money ever paid for a hockey player.

Tommy played left wing. That was the same position Fred had played in Listowel. Since then, he had played point, cover-point, and rover. Ottawa already had players at all those positions. Harry Westwick was the rover. His nickname was

Rat, and he'd been with Ottawa for many years. So had Harvey Pulford and Art Moore, the two defencemen. Alf Smith was another Ottawa veteran. He played right wing. The only open position was centre. Fred was put there, but there were problems from the first practice.

Coach Pete Green was not sure about the newcomers. Ottawa had always played an old-school game. Their style relied on a lot of short passes. Fred liked to burst ahead with his blazing speed. That was all right if he had the puck. It wasn't so good if he did not. The rules at this time didn't allow forward passing. If Fred got ahead of the player with the puck, he was offside. Tommy was fast, but Alf and Rat couldn't keep up with Fred. That had been a major problem when Quebec beat Ottawa 8 to 1.

"Fred Taylor has a beautiful shot," said the Ottawa Journal, "but he is not yet at home with the Ottawa forward line."

Fred never got a chance to get settle in at centre. Before the train carrying the Senators home made it to Ottawa, a decision was made. Marty Walsh would take over at centre. Fred would replace Art on defence. Fred was the cover-point, while Harvey played point. With the Ottawa forwards in front of him, Fred could rush the puck whenever he got a chance. He still had to protect his goalie, but he was so fast he had no trouble getting back to his own end.

Ottawa's second game of the season was on January 11, 1908. It was their first home game of the year. The site was the city's brand new arena on Laurier Avenue. It had space for 7,000 fans. There were seats for 4,500 people. A standing room section could hold 2,500 more. When the Senators played against the Montreal Wanderers, 7,140 people squeezed into

the building. It was the biggest crowd that
had ever seen a hockey game in Ottawa.
The hometown fans cheered as Ottawa
beat their arch-rivals 12 to 2. Marty scored
five goals for Ottawa that night. Tommy
had four. Still, everyone agreed that Fred
was the star.

"Taylor was a tower of strength," said
the *Ottawa Citizen*. "He won roar after
roar of applause with his spectacular
rushes." Twice, Fred raced from end to
end to score goals. "He tore through the
Wanderers team as if he had wings," the
Citizen said. His awesome play made Fred
the idol of the crowds. "He was given
some of the greatest ovations ever given a
hockey player in Ottawa."

Fred never forgot that night. Nearly 60
years later, he wrote about the game for
the *Listowel Banner*. He said it was one of
the highlights of his entire life. Strangely,
though, he remembered the score as 8 to 5

… and he thought that he'd scored five goals!

A lot of stories were written about that game. Many said that Earl Grey was in the crowd. Lord Grey was the Governor General of Canada. He became famous for donating a championship trophy to Canadian football — the Grey Cup. But he was a hockey fan too. The stories claim that he was very impressed by Fred. On his way out of the new arena, Lord Grey said, "He's a cyclone if ever I saw one!"

A reporter from the *Ottawa Free Press* heard the remark. He wrote: "In Portage la Prairie, they called him a tornado. In Houghton, Michigan, he was known as a whirlwind. From now on, he'll be known as Cyclone Taylor."

Did it really happen just like that? Probably not. No one has ever been able to find that article. It may never have been written. As for Lord Grey, it is hard to tell for sure if he was really at that game. It's possible he made the remark after a different game.

No matter how it really happened, one thing is certain: soon after Fred arrived in Ottawa, the legend of Cyclone Taylor was born.

6 The Senators and the Stanley Cup

Now that Cyclone had a flashy nickname, the star player had Senators fans very excited. They hoped he would help bring the Stanley Cup back to Ottawa. But the Senators could not pull away from their rivals from Montreal.

The 1907–08 ECAHA season was only 10 games long. Through the first eight games, the Senators and Wanderers were tied for first place. The team that won their final meeting of the season would be the league champion. The Wanderers were also the defending Stanley Cup champions. This meant that the winner of the ECAHA would get the Stanley Cup too.

The game took place in Montreal on February 29, 1908. It didn't start until 8 o'clock at night, but people began arriving

CHALLENGE THE CHAMPION

In its early days, the Stanley Cup did not belong to any one league. It was a challenge trophy. The champions of the top senior leagues could compete for it. If a team played in the same league as the current champion, they could win the Stanley Cup by beating the champs in the regular-season standings. If a team played in a different league, it had to issue a challenge to the Stanley Cup champions. Then, a special playoff series would be arranged.

three hours earlier. They hoped to buy last-minute tickets. Over 7,000 got in to see the game. Two thousand more were left waiting outdoors. Some of them smashed windows to get inside the arena. Extra police had to be called in to prevent more trouble.

During the season, Cyclone had become the brightest new hockey star in eastern Canada. Art Ross of the Wanderers wasn't far behind. Like Cyclone, Ross played cover-point. He was a big man. He was probably heavier than Cyclone by about 25 pounds. He was also fast — though not as fast as Cyclone — and was skilled and smart. Ross had been embarrassed in the 12 to 2 loss at the start of the season. Now he wanted revenge.

This game was a good one right from the opening faceoff. Both Ross and Cyclone delivered hard hits on defence. They rushed the puck whenever they got the chance. Twice in the first half, Ross sent Cyclone sprawling with solid body checks. Ross was bumped hard too. A smash in the face left him with a bloody nose. Ross wouldn't go off for repairs. He left a trail of red splotches on the ice.

About 10 minutes into the first half, Cyclone picked up the puck. He raced from his own net all the way to the Wanderers' end. Then he slid the puck to his teammate Marty. Marty shot, but the puck was stopped. Ross picked it up and dashed to the Senators' end. He lost it before he could shoot. Harvey, Cyclone's partner at point, scooped up the puck. He brought it back to the Wanderers' end! Harvey made a quick pass to Alf. He sent the puck on to Tommy, who fired a shot on goal. It wasn't a hard shot, but it found the net! The Senators led 1 to 0 when the first half ended.

Play was very rough in the second half. About five minutes in, Wanderers centre

Bruce Stuart got knocked out. He was carried off the ice. Stuart returned to action a few minutes later and scored to tie the game. Then Ross scored to give the Wanderers a 2 to 1 lead. Before long, Alf scored to tie it up for the Senators.

The fans in Montreal were shouting like crazy for their team. The Wanderers answered with another quick goal. Cyclone nearly tied it up again, but his shot was stopped. Then Ross scored again for the Wanderers.

The teams were slowing down, but the rough play continued. Late in the game, Cyclone collided with a Wanderers player. Both went down hard and had to go off the ice. Cyclone was still laying in the dressing room when the game ended. The Wanderers won 4 to 2.

The Stanley Cup was staying in Montreal. Ottawa fans would have to hope for better things next year.

The Senators made many changes before the 1908–09 season. All of the old Ottawa veterans retired. Tommy moved out west and played hockey for a team in Edmonton. The only players left in Ottawa were Cyclone, Marty, and Percy Lesueur, the goalie.

Four new starters were brought in. One of them was Bruce Stuart from the Wanderers. Bruce had played with Cyclone back in Houghton in 1906. Now, he was the Senators' new team captain. The rivalry with the Wanderers was hotter than ever.

Ottawa fans were upset when the Wanderers beat their team in the first game of the 1909 season. Things got a lot better after that. In their second game, the Senators beat Quebec 13 to 5. Then they beat the Montreal Shamrocks 11 to 3. Later, they beat Quebec 18 to 4!

Goals were the only statistic in hockey

THE PROS TAKE OVER

The word "amateur" was dropped from the Eastern Canada Amateur Hockey Association in the 1908–09 season. The league became known as the Eastern Canada Hockey Association. All the players were now professionals.

at this time. Nobody kept track of assists. That meant Cyclone's name didn't show up in the summaries very often. In truth, nearly half of the Senators' goals were owed to him. Cyclone was on fire! No one could skate as fast as he could. No one led such brilliant rushes. He could score goals, or set up his teammates. And he did it all while playing great defence.

The Ottawa Senators' last home game of the season was against the Montreal Wanderers. Once again, the winner would be the league champ and take home the Stanley Cup. But fans in Ottawa were worried. Their star player had been injured a few days before the big game.

It happened during a game against the Montreal Shamrocks. Cyclone was chasing a loose puck behind the net when he fell down. As he did, his right foot got caught in a Shamrock player's skate. There was a loud ripping sound as Cyclone's leather skate tore open. Then blood began gushing onto the ice.

Cyclone suffered a long cut between his heel and his ankle. The cut went right down to the bone. Ottawa's team doctor cleaned the wound and put in stitches. There was a lot of skin left hanging from Cyclone's foot. The doctor simply grabbed a pair of scissors and trimmed it off! Then he sent Cyclone to the hospital.

Cyclone had just four days to get ready for the Wanderers. Would he be able to play? On game night, he wrapped his injured foot in cotton. He wore a special skate with a thick band of leather attached to the outside. The day before, he had told sportswriters, "I can stand any amount of pain when the Stanley Cup is at stake." Could he really?

"In the first few minutes, Taylor limped," reported the *Ottawa Citizen*. "Then, the excitement of the struggle caused Cyclone to forget his injured foot."

Once he got going, Cyclone was as good as ever. He set up Marty for the first goal. Soon after, he scored one himself. He raced all over the ice, leading the Senators to an 8 to 3 victory. The Stanley Cup was coming back to Ottawa!

Senators fans were thrilled. They poured onto the ice when the game was over. Players like Marty and Cyclone were hoisted onto shoulders. Celebrations went on throughout the night.

No one would have believed it then,

but this was the last time Cyclone ever wore the Senators' red, white, and black uniform in Ottawa.

CYCLONE AND STANLEY

Cyclone wanted to take the Stanley Cup to Listowel after Ottawa's 1909 win. He wasn't allowed to. Players didn't get a special day with the Stanley Cup like they do today. Back then, players' names weren't engraved on the Stanley Cup either. So, Cyclone and his teammates scratched their names into the Cup themselves! The name Fred W. Taylor can still be seen on the original Stanley Cup bowl at the Hockey Hall of Fame.

7 Backwards into History

To hockey fans, Cyclone was a hero. To others, he was just a small-town boy from a poor family.

Cyclone had fallen in love with a woman in Ottawa. Her named was Thirza Cook. He wanted to marry Thirza, but her mother did not approve. Cyclone made himself a promise. As soon as he saved $10,000 in the bank, he would marry Thirza. So when a nearby team started offering huge contracts, Cyclone took notice.

The hockey team was in Renfrew, Ontario. Renfrew is a small town about 90 kilometres (56 miles) east of Ottawa. Its hockey teams had been champions for years. Yet, big-city teams never took them seriously. Some of Renfrew's citizens were very wealthy. They felt their town was not getting a fair chance in hockey. They wanted a team that was good enough to win the Stanley Cup.

The team owners made a plan. They would build the best hockey team money could buy for the 1909–10 season. They signed Lester Patrick for $3,000. They gave his younger brother Frank $2,000.

Cyclone was now the biggest name in hockey. He was the star Renfrew really wanted. Contract talks went on for weeks. One day, newspaper articles would say he had jumped to Renfrew. The next, stories claimed he was staying in Ottawa. He finally signed a contract with Renfrew on

December 30, 1909. Cyclone always said that Renfrew paid him $5,250. The exact figures are unclear, but he probably got a $4,000 salary. He also got a new government job worth about $1,200. The combined wage was a huge sum of money at the time.

Now Renfrew had the team they wanted. No hockey team had ever paid such high salaries before. People began calling them the Renfrew Millionaires.

The Millionaires played in a brand new league called the National Hockey Association (NHA). When the Ottawa Senators agreed to join the NHA, it meant the Stanley Cup was really in sight. First, Renfrew would have to finish at the top of the NHA standings. Most experts agreed they could do it.

The Renfrew Millionaires brought in players from across Canada. All of them were very talented. Many, like Cyclone and Lester, were the best wherever they went. In sports, however, talent alone is not enough. It took time for all the stars to learn to work as a team. When they finally got on a roll, it was too late. A loss to the Wanderers late in the season ended their chances at first place.

The main story of the season was the rivalry between Renfrew and Ottawa. Ottawa fans were angry with Cyclone. He was their Stanley Cup hero. They didn't want to him to leave for Renfrew. Now that he had, they turned against him. Cyclone made things even worse for himself. He made a cocky remark to a reporter. He bragged that he would score against Ottawa while skating backwards. He was only joking. The newspaper even said so. All the same, Cyclone's boast made Ottawa fans even angrier.

Renfrew made their first visit to Ottawa on February 12, 1910. The scene at the arena was just like a Stanley Cup match. Fans began arriving four hours before the game. Close to 7,000 people jammed inside — and it seemed like they all came to boo Cyclone.

"Taylor braved the ordeal with a smile," the *Ottawa Citizen* reported. Hometown fans threw things at him. Lemons, limes, and other garbage were tossed onto the ice. Someone even threw a whiskey bottle at him. "I didn't mind the hooting, the hissing or the names they called me," Cyclone told reporters later. "But when that bottle crashed a few yards away, I felt the joke had gone far enough."

The Senators beat Renfrew that night. Cyclone did not score a goal against Ottawa backwards or forward.

Things went much better when the Senators came to Renfrew on March 8. The Millionaires won the game 17 to 2! Cyclone scored three goals. The *Ottawa*

Citizen said the third one "was really shot while the Listowel Cyclone was skating backwards."

There may be more stories about the backwards goal than any other moment in Cyclone's career. Many people swore for the rest of their lives that Cyclone had skated backwards. Not only that, they said he skated from end to end and past the entire Ottawa team!

Cyclone's teammate Lester remembered it differently. He said that Cyclone was skating forward until an Ottawa defenceman hit him. Cyclone was spun around. Then, while skating in reverse, he

NHA TO NHL

In November of 1917, the National Hockey Association broke up and reorganized. It became known as the National Hockey League, or the NHL.

backhanded the puck into the net.

It seems there is truth to the stories of the backwards skating. The *Renfrew Journal* reported: "Taylor got the puck on a pass and was skating in his usual fine fashion. He turned, and going backwards, he skated a piece. Then, he sent the shot home to the Ottawa net with skill and swiftness."

The *Ottawa Evening Journal* told a similar story. It said that Cyclone "skated backwards for a distance of five or six yards, then put the puck through the Ottawa goal."

Cyclone himself would never say for sure how he scored. However it happened, fans in Renfrew were thrilled.

After the season, the Millionaires were invited to New York City. They played an exhibition game there against the Montreal Wanderers. The Wanderers were without two of their best players, and they had to borrow one from Ottawa. Still, it was

IF YOU CAN MAKE IT THERE ...

Cyclone's trip to New York with the Renfrew Millionaires in 1910 was his second visit to the city. His first trip was with the Ottawa Senators in 1909. He was a big hit with the fans that year too. They called him "Little Jeff." That was because he looked like a smaller version of Jim Jeffries, the world heavyweight boxing champion. Cyclone returned to New York with Renfrew in 1911. He played there for the final time in 1914.

another chance for revenge against a top team that had beaten them.

"It was a wonderful exhibition of hockey," said a report from New York in Toronto's *Globe* newspaper. Once again, Cyclone was singled out as the top star. "His end-to-end rushes swept the crowd into enthusiasm. His cyclonic rushes, his sudden stops and his brilliant checking [defeated] the opposing seven."

The Millionaires beat the Wanderers 9 to 4. After the game, American newspapers declared them world champions. It was as close as the tiny town of Renfrew ever came to winning the Stanley Cup.

8 Westward Once Again

The NHA teams began to crack down on salaries. It would be many years before a hockey player earned anything close to $5,000 again. Owners wanted a salary cap for the 1910–11 NHA season. It would limit their spending to $5,000 for an entire team! Cyclone probably made about $1,800 to play in Renfrew that season.

Players like Lester and his brother Frank stayed home that season. They wanted more money to travel across the country.

Instead, the Patrick brothers played hockey with their local team in Nelson, British Columbia. Nelson played in a small local league, but the brothers had big dreams. Soon, they brought important changes to the game of hockey.

The Patricks created a brand new league for the winter of 1911-12. It was called the Pacific Coast Hockey Association (PCHA). Frank and Lester ran the PCHA. They used money from the sale of their father's lumber business to pay for the first artificial ice rinks in Canada. They built one in Vancouver and another in Victoria. Lester was a player with the PCHA team in Victoria. He was also the owner, manager, and coach. Frank had all the same jobs with the PCHA team in Vancouver. He called his team the Millionaires, like the team in Renfrew.

In hockey today, players change teams often. Sometimes they're traded. Often they move as free agents. Some even go back and forth between North America and Europe. When old-time players tried to jump teams, there could be trouble. League officials and team owners acted as if rules were being broken. They wanted to be the ones who controlled where people went. When the PCHA started up, NHA owners expected players to stay put. The Patricks convinced many stars to join their new league, though.

Frank and Lester owned their own teams and their own arenas too. That meant more money from ticket sales could be put towards players' salaries. The salaries were higher than most NHA teams could afford. The NHA owners accused the PCHA of raiding their teams. Frank and Lester said they only signed players who had yet to sign new contracts with their old NHA teams.

"We had Cyclone in mind right from

Cyclone wearing his Vancouver Millionaires uniform

the beginning," Lester admitted.

The Renfrew Millionaires broke up before the 1911–12 season. Cyclone assumed he would become a free agent. He actually wanted to rejoin the Ottawa Senators. The NHA didn't allow it. Former Renfrew players became property of the NHA. Their names were drawn at random and given to other NHA teams. The Wanderers drew Cyclone's name, but he didn't want to go to Montreal. His

MAKING HOCKEY MORE MODERN

The PCHA made hockey a modern sport. It was the first important league to allow forward passing. It was also the first to keep track of assists. Later, it became the first league to have playoffs. This gave more teams a chance to win the Stanley Cup. The PCHA hung onto the rover position, though. The NHA dropped the extra player in 1911–12.

government job was still in Ottawa and so was his girlfriend, Thirza. The Senators tried to work out a trade for Cyclone. The Wanderers wouldn't deal. When Cyclone refused to play for Montreal, the NHA suspended him for the entire season.

Cyclone had been kept off the ice before — when the OHA banned him back in 1905. He didn't like it then, and he liked it even less now. He was nearly 27 years old. In this era, few hockey players played past their thirtieth birthdays. Cyclone was sensitive about his age. He was going bald, which made him look older than he was. Newspapers sometimes called him as "the old man."

The 1912 ban had one big difference from the 1905 ban. Cyclone was much more famous now. He was the biggest star in hockey. For that reason, the NHA wanted to get him back on the ice. So, the Wanderers agreed to let a new NHA team in Toronto sign Cyclone for the 1912–13 season. Ottawa also made a new offer. But Cyclone was still unhappy. "I don't like the idea of being bought and sold by others," he said. "I'm my own man."

He decided to jump to the PCHA.

On November 19, 1912, Frank Patrick made an announcement. Cyclone had signed with the Vancouver Millionaires. His salary was about $2000. Though he was moving clear across the country, Cyclone would keep his government job.

NOT RICH ENOUGH

It was impossible to compete in professional hockey in a town as tiny as Renfrew. The rink there only had 1,500 seats. There was no way to sell enough tickets to pay the team's high salaries. The owners in Renfrew lost about $20,000 chasing their Stanley Cup dream in 1909–10. That would be like losing half-a-million dollars today!

The premier of the province of British Columbia was a hockey fan and had arranged it. Cyclone would work with the Department of Immigration in Vancouver.

During the winter of 1913–14, Cyclone enjoyed his best season yet. Frank moved Cyclone from cover-point to rover. With less defensive duties to worry about, Cyclone became a scoring star. During the 16-game season, Cyclone tied for the league lead with 24 goals. His 15 assists

CYCLONE'S SHORT SEASON

When Cyclone was banned by the OHA for the 1904–05 season, he missed an entire winter of hockey. In 1912, he got to see a little action — by sneaking into a league game with the Senators before he was banned. After the season, he suited up with the NHA all-star team for a three-game series with the PCHA all-stars.

were the most in the league, and he won the PCHA scoring title with 39 points.

After the season, Cyclone made a brief visit to Ottawa. He had finally saved $10,000. It was time to make good on a promise. On March 14, 1914, he finally married Thirza. Then they went back to Vancouver together. A year later, Cyclone brought something else to Vancouver too.

9 Victory in Vancouver

Cyclone played better than ever in the PCHA. His team did not do as well as hoped. During the 1912–13 season, the Millionaires were a distant second in the PCHA standings. In 1913–14, they dropped to third. All that changed the following year. The Millionaires seemed unbeatable that season.

Many early hockey stars called the 1915 Vancouver Millionaires the greatest team they had ever seen. Eleven men played for the Millionaires that year. Seven were later inducted into the Hockey Hall of Fame. The team romped through the season with a record of 13 wins and only four losses. Many of those wins were by lopsided scores. Cyclone had 23 goals in the 16 games he played. He also had a league-leading 22 assists. That gave him a total of 45 points — good enough to win his second straight scoring title.

In 1914, a new championship series began. The champions of the PCHA and NHA champs would fight for the Stanley Cup. The first team to win three out of five games would be the series winner.

HALL-TIME GREATS...

Vancouver's seven Hockey Hall of Fame players from 1914–15 were: Si Griffis, Hugh Lehman, Mickey MacKay, Frank Nighbor, Frank Patrick, Barney Stanley, and Cyclone Taylor.

Since it took a whole week to travel across the country by train, the entire series was held in one city. Vancouver hosted the series in 1915. Their opponents were Cyclone's old team: the Ottawa Senators. There was no one left on the Ottawa team who had played with Cyclone back in 1909. However, there were some familiar faces. His former teammate Alf Smith was the coach of the Senators. The team's new cover-point was someone else Cyclone knew well. It was Art Ross, former star of the Montreal Wanderers.

Game one of the Stanley Cup series was played on March 22, 1915. It was played under PCHA rules. That meant there were seven players on the ice. Also, forward passing was allowed. The Senators had trouble adjusting to this modern rule.

"Ottawa tried the forward pass," the Vancouver *Province* reported, "but they did not make much success of it." The paper went on to claim that "western players, not western rules" were the real difference. Vancouver won the game 6 to 2.

Ross was the only Ottawa player who could break through the Vancouver defence. He also kept a close eye on Cyclone, but Ross could not stop his old rival. "Taylor dazzled Ottawa with his great rushes," reported the Vancouver *Province*. "They checked him as closely as possible, but they could not prevent him from getting goals."

Game two was on March 24. NHA rules were used this time. That meant there would be no forward passing and no rover. Coach Alf Smith promised that the Senators would play much better under familiar rules. Team manager Frank Shaughnessy said so too — and they did. The Senators came out flying.

The team from Ottawa scored two goals in the first period. They seemed to have things under control. Then, just 55 seconds into the second period, Mickey MacKay got the Millionaires on the board. Six minutes later, Vancouver right winger Frank Nighbor stole the puck near centre ice. Frank dropped a pass for Cyclone, who sped down into the Ottawa end. He blasted the puck into the net and the score was tied 2 to 2. Before the second period ended, Cyclone set up another goal. Then he scored two more himself. The Millionaires went on to win the game 8 to 3.

Nobody really expected the Senators to bounce back. But nobody expected what happened in game three either. After a close first period, the Millionaires romped to a 12 to 3 victory! Barney Stanley scored five goals. Cyclone set up one of them, and added three more himself.

The Vancouver Millionaires were Stanley Cup champions. Though it was a team effort, the *Vancouver World* gave credit to Cyclone. "He is undoubtedly the best hockey player in the world," the newspaper said. "His marvelous skating and stickhandling ability completely demoralized the Senators."

The Senators' manager agreed. "Cyclone Taylor was the best hockey player in the world when he left Ottawa," Frank Shaughnessy said. "If possible, he is even better now. He is amazing."

Cyclone kept amazing people during the 1915–16 season. The Millionaires slumped that year, but Cyclone didn't. He won his third straight scoring title with 22 goals and 13 assists for 35 points in 18 games. He scored six goals in a single game!

Things didn't go quite as well the next year. Cyclone had gotten sick when he first came to Vancouver. He missed several games during the 1912–13 season because of appendicitis. He should have had an operation to remove his appendix, but didn't. By the start of the 1916–17 season, the pain was too much to bear. Early in the morning on December 12, 1916, Cyclone was rushed to the hospital. A few hours later, he went into surgery. Newspapers across Canada reported on his condition. They said he would be fine, but he missed nearly seven weeks of action. "Old man appendicitis accomplished what hockey players have failed to do in the past," said the Vancouver *News Advertiser*. "He put Cyclone Taylor down and made him stay down."

Down but not done! Cyclone was healthy again for the next season. Both he and the Millionaires had another huge year. In 18 games, he had a career high 32 goals. No other player in the PCHA scored more than 20 goals that year. With 11 assists, Cyclone's total of 43 points was good enough for his fourth scoring title. Not only that, he went through the entire season without getting a single penalty.

The Millionaires won the very first PCHA playoff. They were back on top of the league. Now it was off to Toronto for the Stanley Cup Final. It was the first time that Cyclone had played in Toronto since the 1904 OHA junior championship. He was given a nice welcome back. The local newspapers didn't give his team much of a chance, though. The Toronto players were bigger and younger. They played a tougher style than Vancouver did, and they were almost as fast.

The NHA had become the National Hockey League (NHL) that season. Game one of the Stanley Cup Final was played under NHL rules. That meant six players instead of seven and no forward passing. Vancouver and Toronto took turns winning during the first four games. The series was tied 2 to 2. Cyclone had scored eight goals!

Game five was not just the last game of the series, it was also the best game. The

Millionaires planned to make the most of their speed. Cyclone and Mickey played very well. "It is doubtful," Toronto's *Globe* reported, "if MacKay and Taylor ever worked so hard."

Cyclone scored his ninth goal of the series in the third period. Still, Toronto had a 2 to 1 lead late in the game. Vancouver refused to give up. "The remaining six minutes were tense with excitement," the *Toronto Star* reported. "The Millionaires threw everybody on the attack."

ASSISTS WERE RARE

There are two main reasons why there were so few assists during Cyclone's days in the PCHA: Forward passing was only allowed between the two blue lines. It was not allowed inside either team's zone. And only one player received an assist on any goal scored. Nowadays, two assists are given out on almost every goal.

Toronto's defence would not crack. Vancouver fired shot after shot, but no one scored again. Toronto won 2 to 1.

There would be no Stanley Cup celebration in Vancouver in 1918. In fact, no Vancouver team has won the Stanley Cup since 1915.

10 The Legend Lives On

Cyclone turned 33 years old in June of 1918. He was now a father too. His hockey career was winding down, but he still had some great games left in him. In the 1918–19 season, Cyclone led the PCHA in scoring for the fifth time.

Cyclone and Thirza eventually had five children: Fred Jr., John, Edward, Mary, and Joan. Cyclone knew Thirza wanted him to retire, but he couldn't bring himself to quit just yet. He suited up for a handful of games over the next few seasons before finally ending his playing career in 1922.

Cyclone's last great moment on ice came on March 11, 1921. It was the final game of the 1920–21 season. He scored three goals that night, leading Frank Patrick's Vancouver Millionaires to an 11 to 8 victory over Lester Patrick's Victoria team.

"He went out like a champion," Lester said. "I expected nothing less of him."

After he retired from hockey, Cyclone continued to work for the Department of Immigration. Just as he thought, his job in the civil service turned into a full-time career. He stayed with his job well past his hockey playing days. In 1930, he was named commissioner of British Columbia and the Yukon. In 1946, he was awarded the King's Medal for his immigration work during World War II. While working in London in 1947, he met King George — and the future Queen Elizabeth — at

Buckingham Palace. In 1949, he was honoured again for his lengthy service to Canada's Department of Immigration. This time he was named a Member of the Order of the British Empire.

Cyclone finally retired from his job in 1950 — 28 years after he retired from hockey. He was never far from the game he loved, though. His two oldest sons both played hockey while they grew up in Vancouver. Fred Jr. was a pretty good player, but the pressure of being Cyclone's first son made it hard for him to enjoy the game. John helped the University of Toronto hockey team win two college championships in the 1930s. The Toronto Maple Leafs showed interest in him, but Cyclone and Thirza wanted him to stay in school. He graduated as a lawyer in 1940. (In the early 1980s, a member of Cyclone's family did make it to the NHL. It was his grandson Mark Taylor.)

In 1936, Cyclone was named president of the Pacific Coast Hockey League — one of hockey's top minor leagues. He held that job until 1940. After NHL president Frank Calder died in 1943, newspapers reported that Cyclone might take over his job. He never did. Later, he became the honorary president of the British Columbia Amateur Hockey Association. Every now and then, he would suit up and play in old-timers' games.

In 1945, the Hockey Hall of Fame began to select players to honour. Only

Cyclone back on the ice for an old-timers' game.

people who were no longer living were inducted that year. Cyclone was one of the first living people to be inducted into the Hall of Fame in 1947. In 1960, he joined the selection committee. Later that year, he was given another honour. He dug the first shovelful of earth on the site where the original Hall of Fame was built.

Cyclone was active in his work with the Hall of Fame. He gathered information and memorabilia from other hockey stars and their families. He travelled from his home in Vancouver to the Hall in Toronto every year for meetings and induction ceremonies. When he did, he usually paid a visit to Listowel. The townsfolk there never forgot him. He often visited Tara too. After Thirza died in 1963, these trips became even more important to Cyclone. One of the last trips he made to Listowel was in 1975. That summer, the town of Listowel was having its one hundredth birthday. Cyclone raised the town's new flag at the celebration. That same year, he was also inducted into Canada's Sports Hall of Fame.

Cyclone was always well remembered in Vancouver too. When the Vancouver Canucks joined the NHL in 1970, he was invited to the first game. Cyclone posed for pictures with the Stanley Cup. He got a huge cheer from the crowd. He became a regular in the stands at Canucks games over the next few years. In 1977, Cyclone dropped the puck for the ceremonial faceoff when Vancouver hosted the NHL All-Star Game.

Cyclone remained healthy and active until almost the end of his life. His health finally began to go downhill after he suffered a broken hip in 1978. He passed away in Vancouver on June 9, 1979. Later that year, the Canucks renamed their MVP award the Cyclone Taylor Trophy. That award is just one of the many ways that Cyclone is remembered today.

Junior hockey teams in British Columbia have been competing for the Cyclone Taylor Cup as their championship trophy since 1967. There is also a Cyclone Taylor Arena in the Vancouver suburbs. In 1972, the new junior hockey team in Listowel was named the Listowel Cyclones. Today, every team in all levels of the Listowel Minor Hockey Association is called the Cyclones. In 2005, the town of Tara renamed its rink the Cyclone Taylor Arena. Minor hockey teams there were known as the Tara Cyclones during the winter of 2007.

It has been more than 100 years since Cyclone's career began. His name still has its place in hockey. Sadly, few people today really know why that is. Once, he was the most famous hockey player in the world. Now, even those who play on the teams and in the arenas that are named after him know little about Cyclone. Outside of places like Tara, Listowel, and Vancouver, he's hardly known at all anymore. It's a shame. For the people who do know his story, Fred "Cyclone" Taylor will always be a star. He is one of the pioneers that made his sport what it is today. His legend deserves to live on for as long as hockey is played.

Glossary

Amateur: A person who is not paid money to do something, such as playing a sport. Today, people often use this word to mean someone who is not very good at something.

Assist: A pass that leads to a teammate scoring a goal.

Civil service: The many different sections of a country's government. People who work in the Civil service are known as Civil servants. They are not elected. They are hired to do their jobs.

Body check: To stop an opponent from getting the puck by hitting him or her with the hips or shoulders.

Deke: To briefly pretend to move in one direction in order to trick an opponent into going the wrong way.

Disc: Another word for puck.

Exhibition game: A game that is not part of the regular season.

Faceoff: To drop the puck between two opposing centres to restart play after the game has been stopped.

Junior hockey: Amateur hockey was usually divided into three levels. Junior hockey was the lowest level. Junior players were often younger than those at the higher levels.

League: A collection of sports teams that compete against one another at different levels.

Official: A person who makes sure the rules of the game are followed.

Offside: When a player enters the opposing team's zone ahead of the puck.

Opponent: The challenging, or rival, player or team.

Penalty: The punishment of a player for breaking rules by removing the player from the game for a period of time.

Point/Cover-Point: In the early days of hockey, defencemen were called point and cover-point. Usually, the point player stayed closer to his own goalie than the cover-point.

Professional: A person who is paid money to do a job or play a sport. Today, people often use this word to mean someone who is very good at something.

Rover: In the early days of hockey, there were seven players on the ice. The rover lined up between the forwards and the defencemen. The rover could drop back to help play defence or head up ice to join the other forwards on the attack.

Senior hockey: Amateur hockey was usually divided into three levels. Senior hockey was the highest level.

Slashing: To hit an opponent with a hockey stick.

Spectator: A person viewing the game.

Stickhandling: To control the puck with a hockey stick by shifting it from one side of the blade to the other.

Acknowledgements

In a way, I became a writer because of Cyclone Taylor. After learning about him at the Hockey Hall of Fame, and reading Eric Whitehead's biographies of him and the Patrick brothers, I got an idea for a story. This became my 1992 novel, *Hockey Night in the Dominion of Canada*. So, I thought I knew Cyclone's story as well as anyone and that this book would be easy to write. It wasn't. I needed a lot of help putting the pieces together.

Fortunately, there were a lot of people who could help me. Ann-Marie Collins and Sue Schlorff of the Bruce County Museum in Southampton helped with Cyclone's early life in Tara. Kathy Wideman and Sonia Robin of the Listowel Archives had wonderful records of Cyclone's years there. After a few exchanges of emails, Jason Beck from the

Acknowledgements

British Columbia Sports Hall of Fame in Vancouver was kind enough to send me copies of newspaper articles that his organization has on file.

Emails and the regular mail also kept me in touch with several colleagues from the Society for International Hockey Research. Paul Kitchen, Bill Fitsell, and Frank Cosentino were all very generous with their time and their resources. Bill Sproule, who teaches at Michigan Tech University in Houghton, and whose family comes from Thessalon, Ontario, provided me with some rare and useful information.

Thanks also to Rebecca Sjonger for her editorial skills and to Maryann Thomas of the Ginger Press in Owen Sound who said, "write about Cyclone Taylor!" Thank you to Catherine MacIntosh and Erin Winzer at Lorimer. A special thank you to Hadley Dyer, who brought me on board. Hadley, it won't be as much fun without you.

About the Author

ERIC ZWEIG is a managing editor with Dan Diamond and Associates, consulting publishers to the NHL. He has written about sports and sports history for many major publications, including the *Toronto Star* and the *Globe and Mail*. He has also been a writer/producer with CBC Radio Sports and TSN SportsRadio, and written several popular books about hockey for both adults and children. He lives in Owen Sound, Ontario, with his family.

Photo Credits

BC Sports Hall of Fame and Museum: p. 46, p. 75, p. 94, front cover top, front cover bottom, back cover top, back cover bottom

Stratford–Perth Archives: p. 20, back cover middle